MINSTREL BANJO
BRIGGS' BANJO INSTRUCTOR

Performance Notes and Transcriptions by JOSEPH WEIDLICH

Cover of the first complete method published for t...
The "Briggs' Banjo Instructor" (1855) By Thomas F. Briggs

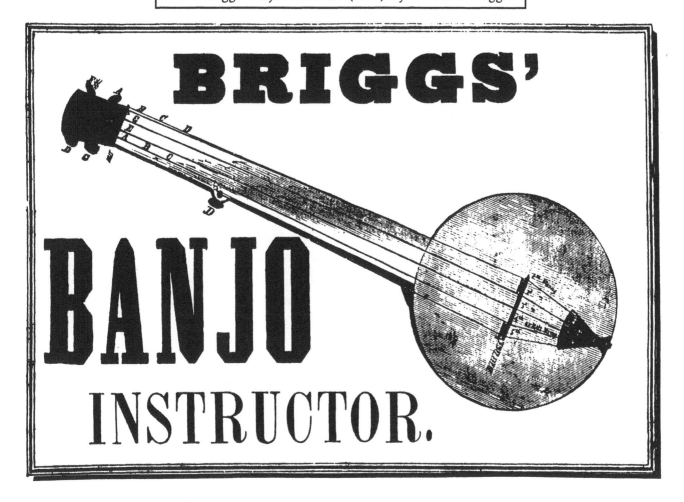

BRIGGS' BANJO INSTRUCTOR.

Cover Art
William Sidney Mount (1807-1868)
The Banjo Player, 1855
Gift of Mr. and Mrs. Ward Melville, 1955
The Museums at Stony Brook

ISBN 1-57424-040-4
SAN 683-8022

Music Notation: Kenneth Warfield
Layout: Cindy Middlebrook
Production: Ron Middlebrook

Copyright © 1997 CENTERSTREAM Publishing
P.O. Box 17878 - Anaheim Hills, CA 92817

Joseph Weidlich

Joseph Weidlich began his formal musical studies on the classic guitar. He moved to Washington, D. C. in 1972, from his native St. Louis, to teach classic guitar. He performed in several classic guitar master classes conducted by notable students of Andres Segovia (i.e., Sr. Jose Tomas [Spain], Oscar Ghiglia [Italy] and Michael Lorimer [U.S.]).

In 1987, he completed research on and writing of an article on Battuto Performance Practice in *Early Italian Guitar Music (1606-1637)*, for the Journal of the Lute Society of America, 1978 (Volume XI). This article outlines the various strumming practices, with numerous examples, found in early guitar methods published in Italy and Spain in the early 17th century. In the late 1970s he published a series of renaissance lute transcriptions for classic guitar, published by DeCamera Publishing Company, Washington, D.C., which were distributed by G. Schirmer, New York/London.

The banjo has been no stranger in Joe's musical life. He began learning folk styles in the early 1960s during the folk music boom later playing plectrum and classic banjo styles. His current research in minstrel banjo demonstrates how that style formed the foundation of contemporary clawhammer banjo. Most recently he has collaborated with banjo builder Mike Ramsey of Appomattox, Virginia, in designing a prototype minstrel banjo based on the dimensions described in Phil Rice's *Correct Method* [1858] as well as similar instruments made by William Boucher in Baltimore in the 1840s.

Table of Contents

Songs

Welcome to the minstrel banjo fraternity!

The year is 1855, 12 years after the first minstrel performance by The Virginia Minstrels in New York City. The banjo has become popular due to its continual exposure in minstrel performances in circuses and theaters. Louis Moreau Gottschalk's new piano song, The Banjo, Grotesque Fantasie, is sweeping the nation. The first published method, Gumbo Chaff's (aka Elias Howe) The Complete Preceptor for the Banjo is issued in 1851, but it contains only very rudimentary information regarding tuning of the banjo and its scale, but no explicit information on the idiomatic right/left hand techniques. While the repertoire it contains is authentic minstrel music, mostly from the repertoire of The Christy Minstrels, the songs are not really "arranged" for the banjo but transposed to the suitable banjo keys of the day (G and D). This is the background for Tom Briggs' Banjo Instructor, published in 1855 by Oliver Ditson (Boston):

> *"Briggs' Banjo Instructor: Containing the elementary principles of music, together with examples and lessons, necessary to facilitate the acquirement of a perfect knowledge of the instrument to which is added a choice collection of pieces, numbering over fifty popular dances, polkas, melodies, &c. &c., many of which have never before been published.*
>
> *Composed and arranged expressly for this work by Thomas F. Briggs."[1]*

Ditson states in the preface to the Briggs method that he was solicited to publish it by Tom Briggs' friends shortly after the death of Briggs (apparently in California). This is the first complete published method for the banjo, which was considered at the time "a mystery unlearnable, and for which music has never before been written." Briggs' method "contains many choice plantation melodies which the author learned when at the south from the negroes, which have never before been published--thus forming a rare collection of quaint old dances, &c..." This statement implies that some of the repertoire contained in his method is based on what Briggs learned directly from the slaves. Most of the 68 songs in the method are banjo solos, which are presented in this edition.

The "Elementary Principles of Music" begin on page 5, followed by specific instructions (contained on pages 8-10,12-13, and 30). Let's eavesdrop and learn from one of the earliest masters of the banjo:

> ## Manner of Holding the Banjo
>
> *"The Banjo should be placed transversely on the right thigh, the right fore arm resting upon the edge of the instrument, the hand hanging above the strings so as to bring the wrist just over the bridge. The head of the Banjo should be elevated so as to bring it nearly even with the left shoulder."*

---

[1] A facsimile edition is available from Tuckahoe Music, Post Office Box 146, Bremo Bluff, VA 23022.

The Left Hand

"The left hand should lightly press the neck just below the Nut, between the thumb and the first finger, leaving the ends of the thumb and fingers free. The arm should hang naturally, with the elbow separated from the body; the fingers should be separated and held ready to strike the strings perpendicularly. The thumb is some-time[s] used to stop the fourth string."

The Right Hand

"The thumb should be extended and rest on the 5th string. The fingers should not be separated, but held closely together, and move simultaneously with the first finger; the first finger should be held a little farther out from the hand than the other fingers. The fingers should be held stiff, except at the 3rd joint. The wrist should be held limber."

Manner of Playing

"In playing, the thumb and first finger only of the right hand are used; the 5th string is touched by the thumb only, this string is always played open, the other strings are touched by the thumb and the first finger ... the strings are touched by the ball of the thumb, and the nail of the 1st finger. The first finger should strike the strings with the back of the nail and then slide to. When using the thumb, the first finger nail should rest against the 1st string; when using the first finger, the thumb should rest on the 5th string; when the first finger strikes any one of the strings, other than the 1st string, the finger should slide to, and rest on the next string to the one struck; when the 1st string is struck, the finger should slide to, and rest on the top of the instrument."

The above descriptions outline the playing positions used in contemporary clawhammer banjo. In fact, many of the idiomatic techniques taken for granted by today's clawhammer banjo enthusiasts were actually developed by the first generation of minstrel banjoists, including use of "G" tuning, alternate string pulloffs, brushes, drop thumb technique, the foundation of melodic style and the "bumm-titty" strum (popularized by banjoist Pete Seeger).

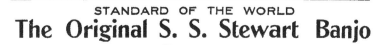

Tom Briggs lists five principal movements, or rhythmic patterns, which form the "basis of all Banjo pieces." They consist of the use of the fifth string alternating with a melodic note; use of double thumbing; and two examples of a dotted eighth note followed by a triplet (often condensed into a one beat motif as well):

Figure 1

(a)

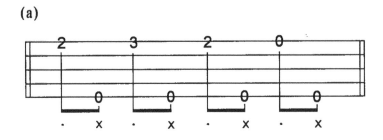

(b)

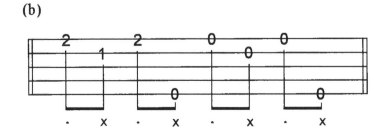

(c)

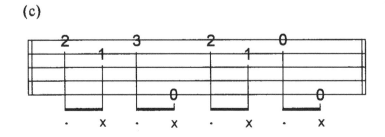

(d)

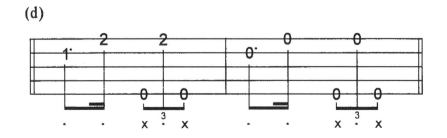

(e)

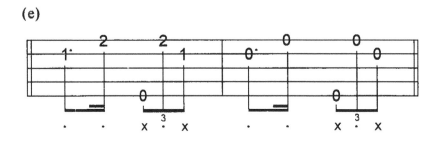

6

Figure 2

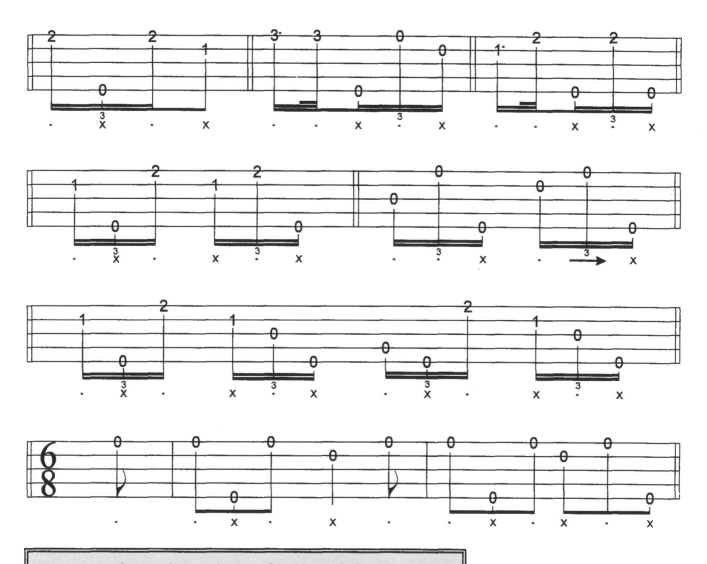

(editor's suggestions are in brackets)

Figure 3

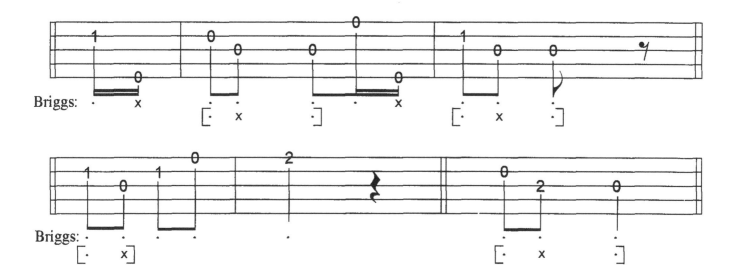

Chords

Briggs states than "when a single chord appears, it is to be played by the first finger alone, which is done by sliding the finger rapidly over the strings, beginning with the lowest note" (i.e., 4th to 1st).

"When two or more chords composed of the same letters occur, the first is made with the first finger, and the second is made by sliding the back of the nail of the thumb rapidly over the strings, commencing with the upper note of the chord" (1st to 4th).

Figure 4

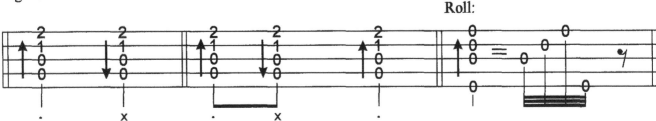

Slurs

(a) Descending Slurs

Briggs describes 2-note descending slurs (the second note being an open string) which occur on the same string (after the first stopped note is played, the second note is "pulled" open by the finger with which the initial note was stopped). Notes to be slurred are indicated by a curved slur line above or below the notes.

Figure 5

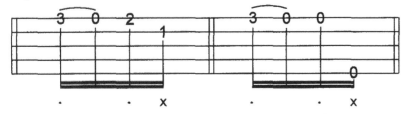

(b) Ascending Slurs

A 2-note ascending slur on the same string, indicated by a curved slur line above or below the notes, is executed by playing the first note with the right hand thumb or finger, then forcefully bringing the left hand finger (usually the middle finger) down on the fingerboard to stop the next note.

Figure 6

8

> *3-note patterns on adjacent strings (e.g., traids, usually played as a triplet) are played by striking the lowest note with the first finger, then sliding the first finger over the remaining notes.*

Figure 7

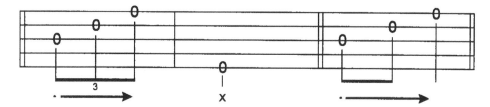

> *A combination right hand finger slide and ascending slur across the first two strings is also found in Briggs. The index finger, as part of the stroke, slides from the second to the first string which segues into an ascending slur.*

Figure 8
Basic Stroke

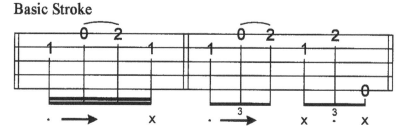

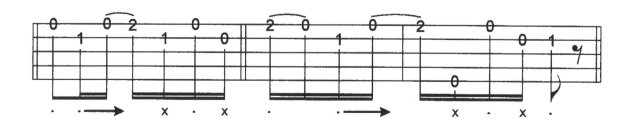

> *Briggs also provides opportunities to use a combination stroke which often consists of a 3-note figure on two adjacent strings, the third note of which is a repeat of the initial note. The initial two notes are played with a nail glide; the last one with the thumb.*

Figure 9

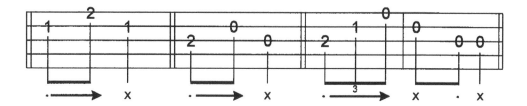

In addition to playing triadic triplets, nail glides can be used in a variety of situations to subtly shift the accent:

Figure 10   Briggs: *Dance, Boatman, Dance* (editor's suggestions)

Figure 11   Additional usages:

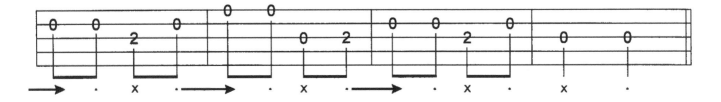

Other Comments

As the thumb is not usually used to play notes on the first string, when Briggs indicates an "x" for the open first string, he implies to play its unison on the second string. Except when used as an aid in tuning the banjo use of unison notes is rare in the early minstrel banjo methods until the mid-1860's.

Figure 12   Use of Unison Notes

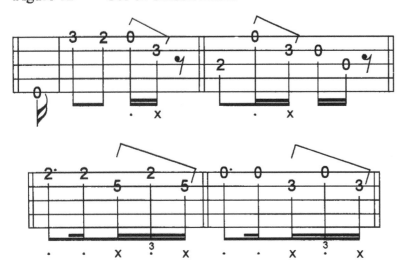

Figure 13   Examples of thumb (T) usage on the bass string.

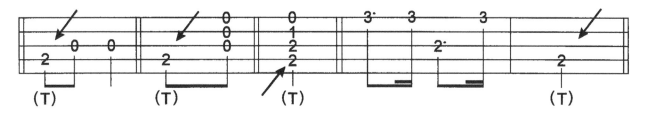

Figure 14   Repeated note examples (editor's interpretation)
Briggs:

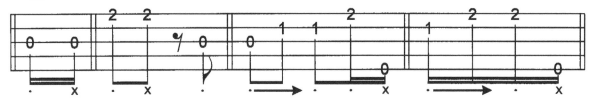

Figure 15   Off beat slurs.

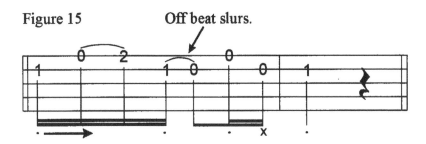

Figure 16

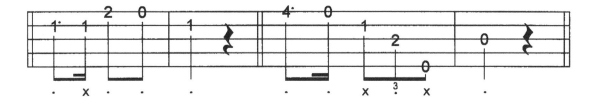

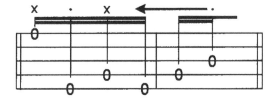

Concluding Comments

The banjo in common usage at the time was fretless.

Using the fifth string as a melodic note is common throughout the minstrel repertoire.

When the note on the first string/fifth fret is notated in Briggs' score, it is usually played open on the fifth string (as it is a unison note); if two appear in succession as part of the same beat the usual practice is to play the first one on the fifth fret of the first string, the second on the fifth string open.

When a song begins with a pickup note(s) (i.e., anacrusis), then a modified first ending has to be constructed (sometimes from as early as the 4th measure of the initial phase). For the most part I have incorporated such endings in the transcriptions.

Briggs states that "the 1st string is the only one ordinarily used in the 2nd position" (notes above the fifth fret). Customary minstrel banjo second position begins at the 5th fret and ends at the 10th fret.

Briggs recommends retuning of the banjo for variety's sake. You would use the same left hand fingerings but the pitch of the banjo would be higher or lower.

The remaining pieces in Briggs are parlor songs arranged for voice with banjo accompaniment. These are played in the "guitar" style (i.e., played in the style of right hand guitar technique in which the thumb played notes on the fifth and fourth strings, third string played by the index finger, second string by the middle finger and first string by the ring finger).

The preface mentions that Briggs used a metal finger pick ("thimble") for "stroke" (banjo-style) play. Thimbles are illustrated in Frank Converse's <u>New and Complete Method for the Banjo With or Without A Master</u>, and in more textual detail by S.S. Stewart, noted Philadelphia banjo manufacturer, in his various discourses later in the 19th century. Use of the thimble probably explains why many of the single note melodic passages in Briggs are played with the index finger. (This performance practice is still used in contemporary clawhammer style although the middle finger is often used in place of the index finger.)

Transposition Data. The songs in Briggs are in the keys of G and D. The fingerings in the key of G correspond to those in modern C tuning while the fingerings of D correspond to those in modern G tuning. Therefore the transposition keys in this edition are C and G respectively

Additional information on the techniques of the minstrel banjoists (covering the period 1851-1865), their arranging techniques, etc., can be found in my book, "The Early Minstrel Banjo: Its Technique and Repertoire."

BANJO THIMBLES
For stroke playing, old style, German silver . . price, each, $0.10

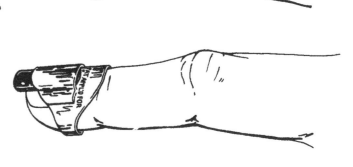

BANJO THIMBLES
New style, Stewart's patent, German silver, with tortoise shell
striking piece . . . . · price, each, $0.30

Notes on the Tablature

In order to reach a wider audience, I have used standard banjo tablature over modern staff notation, even though modern staff notation is used in the minstrel banjo methods. The contemporary banjo tuning of gCGBD should be used (except where notated to raise the fourth string one whole note, from C to D). This interval structure is the same as the minstrel banjo tuning used by Briggs: dGDF#A. The top line of the staff represents the first string, the bottom line the fifth string. Rhythm markings conform to standard usage.

In this edition, I have used an "x" in the tablature to indicate use of right hand thumb. While Briggs used an "F" to indicate use of the first finger, I have used the more conventional "." to indicate this usage.

I have notated nail glide strokes by an arrow: · ⟶

As Briggs does not provide right hand fingerings for all notes in his method, I have included minstrel-style fingerings where I felt it was necessary.

ALABAMA JOE,

This minstrel song folio cover, published by Henry Prentiss of Boston in 1840, gave northerners an early lithographic image of the professional minstrel, posed with his typically long, scroll-peghead banjo. "Alabama Joe" was sung by A.L. Thayer of the Guinea Minstrels, but it is not clear whether the illustration represents Thayer.

- James F. Bollman Collection

ALABAMA JOE

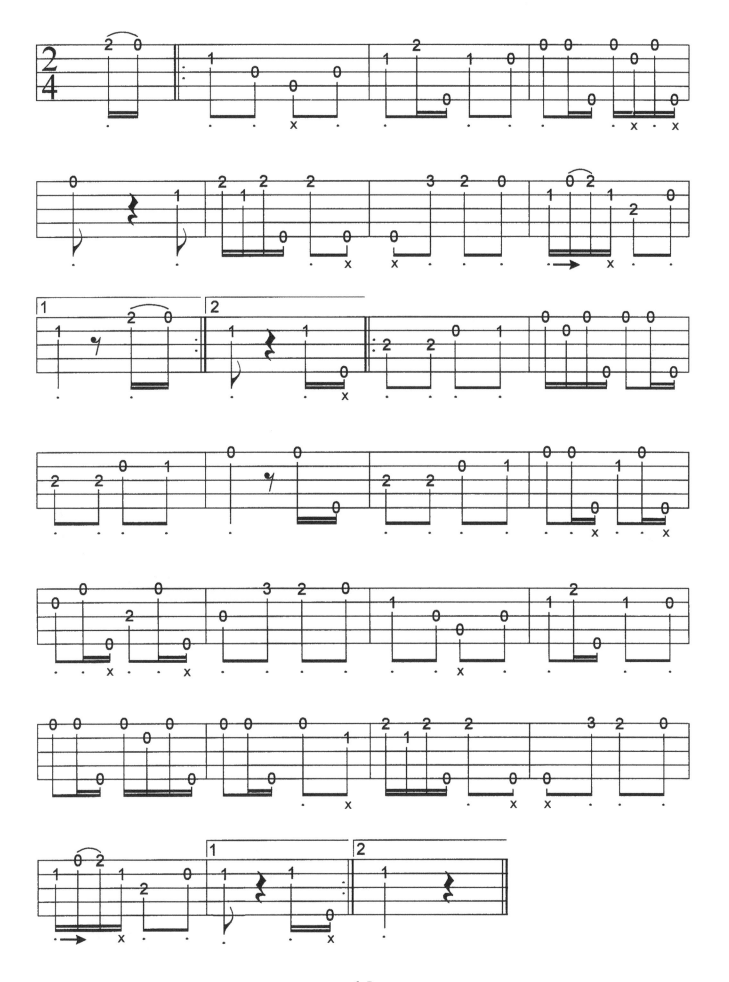

15

BRIGGS' BREAKDOWN

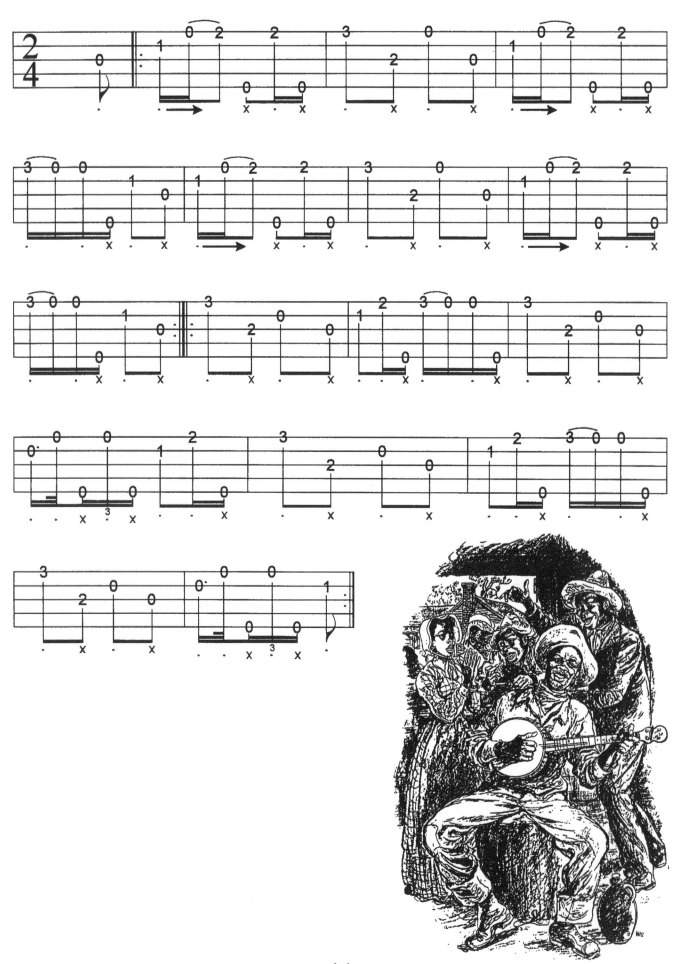

BRIGGS' CORN SCHUCKING JIG

BRIGGS' JIG

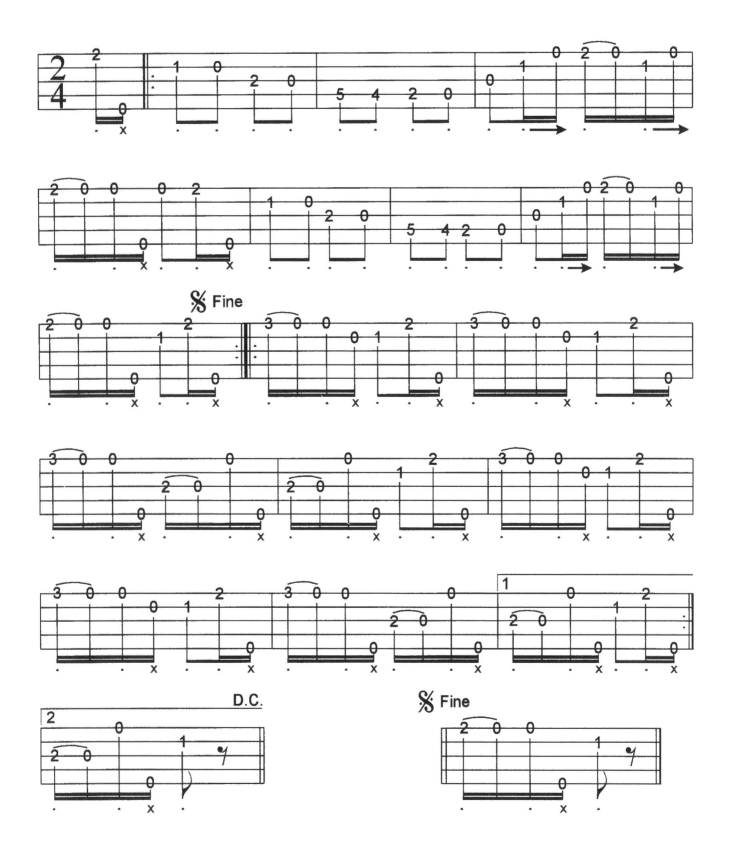

BRIGGS' REEL

CAMPTOWN HORNPIPE

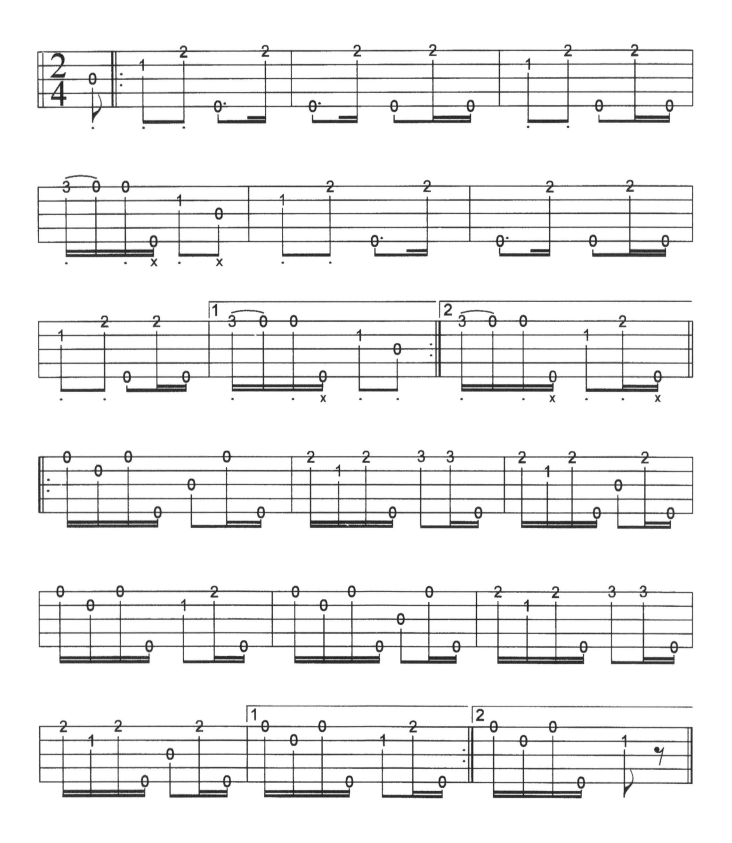

CARNEY JIG

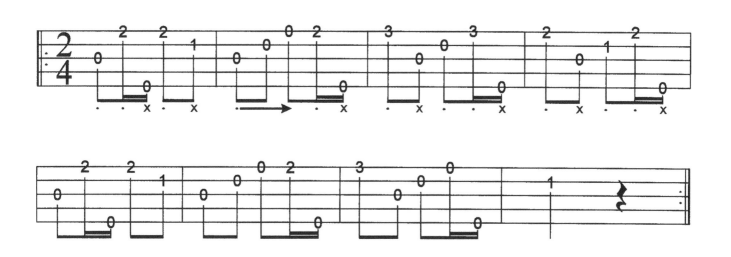

CARRY ME BACK TO OLD VIRGINNY

CIRCUS JIG

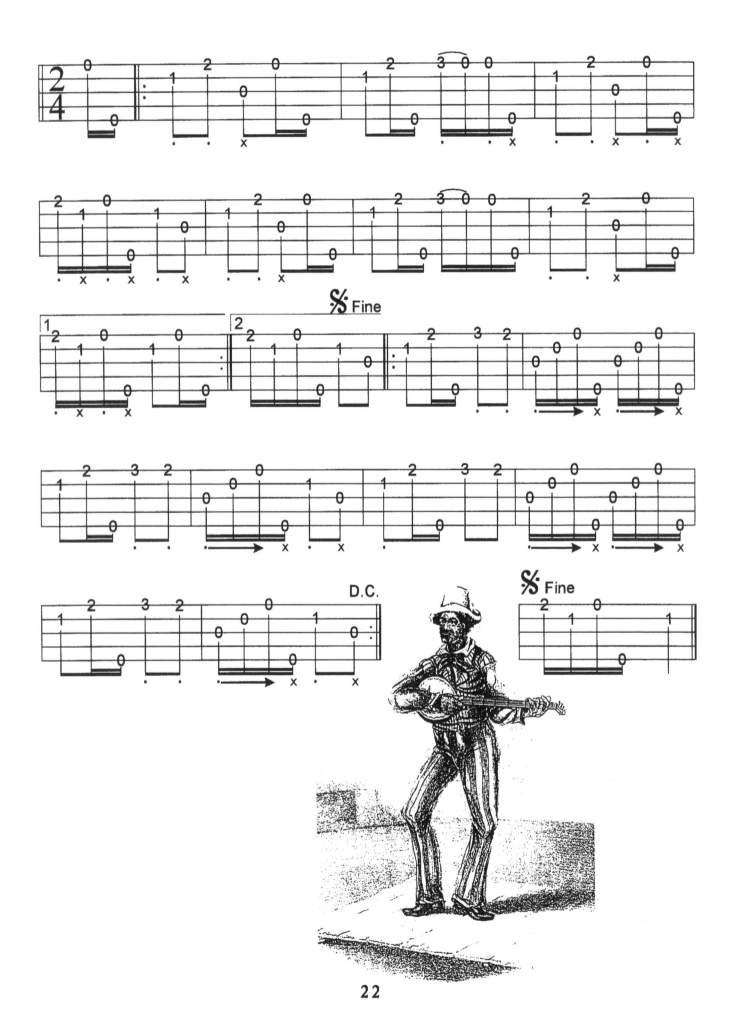

THE CONGO PRINCE JIG

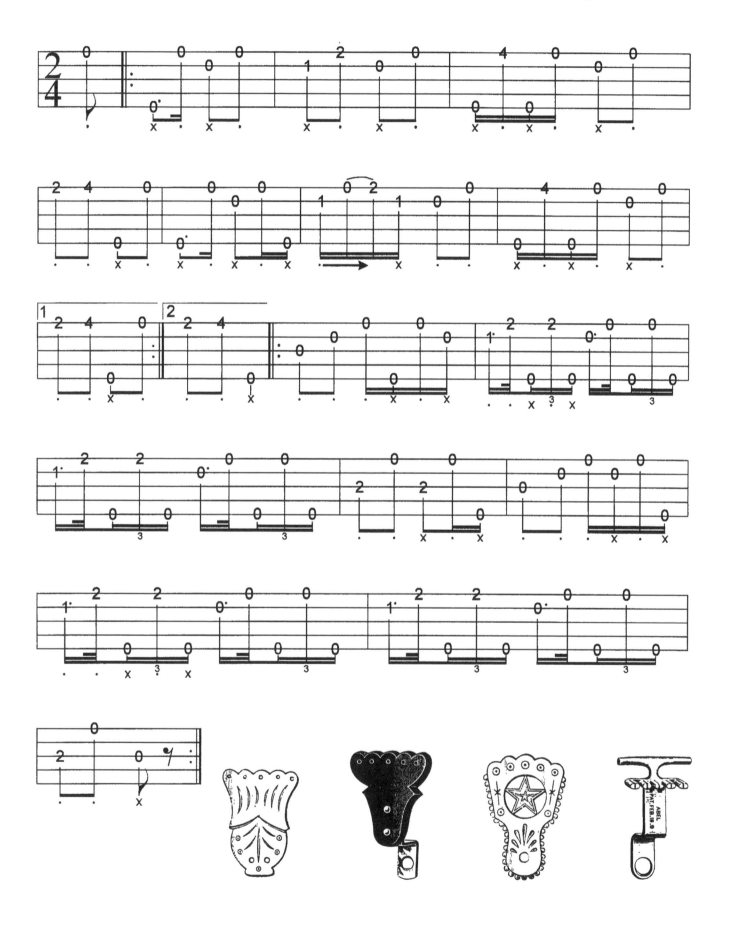

DANCE, BOATMAN, DANCE

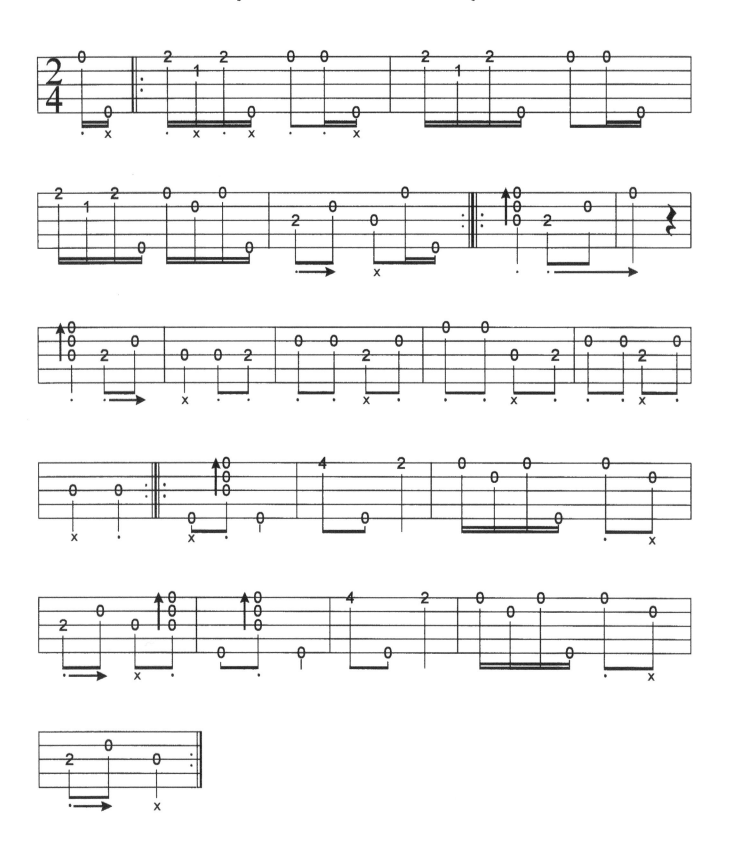

DANDY JIM

DARKEY FISHER'S HORNPIPE

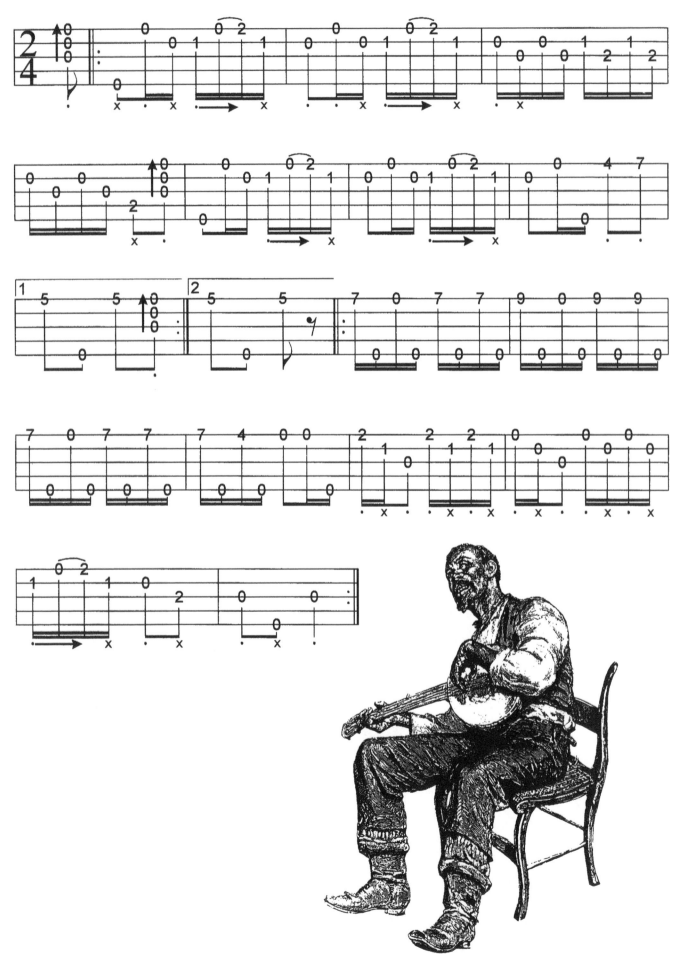

DARKEY MONEY MUSK

DEAREST MAE

DE BONES IN DE BARNYARD

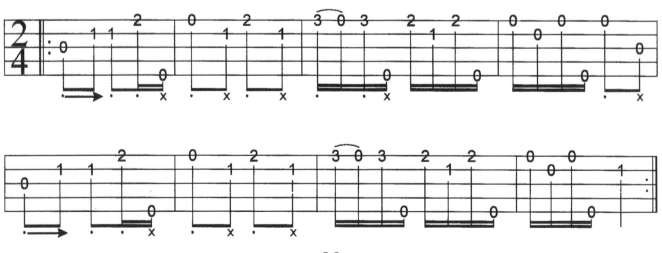

DE GAL WID DE BLUE DRESS ON

ETHIOPIAN CRACOVIENNE

EPHRIAM'S LAMENT

GIT UP IN DE MORNIN

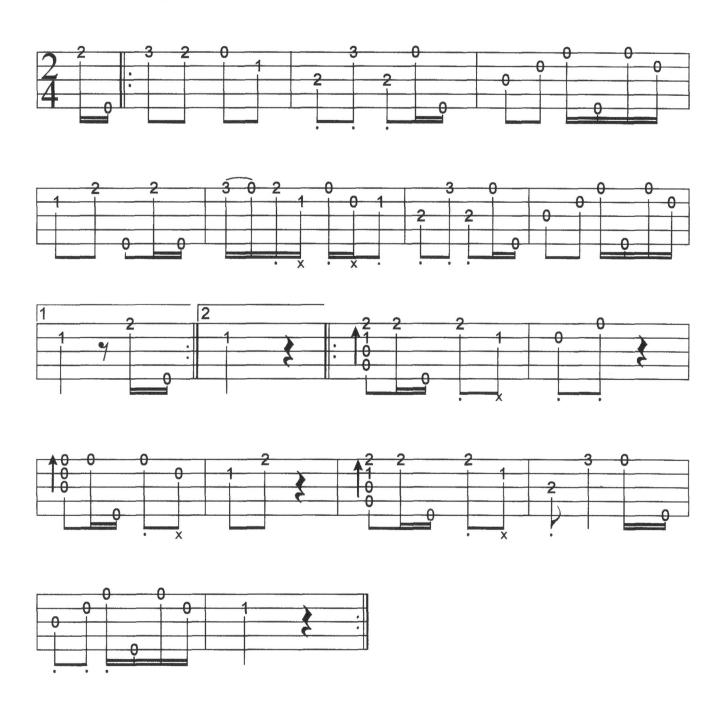

GOING OBER DE MOUNTAIN

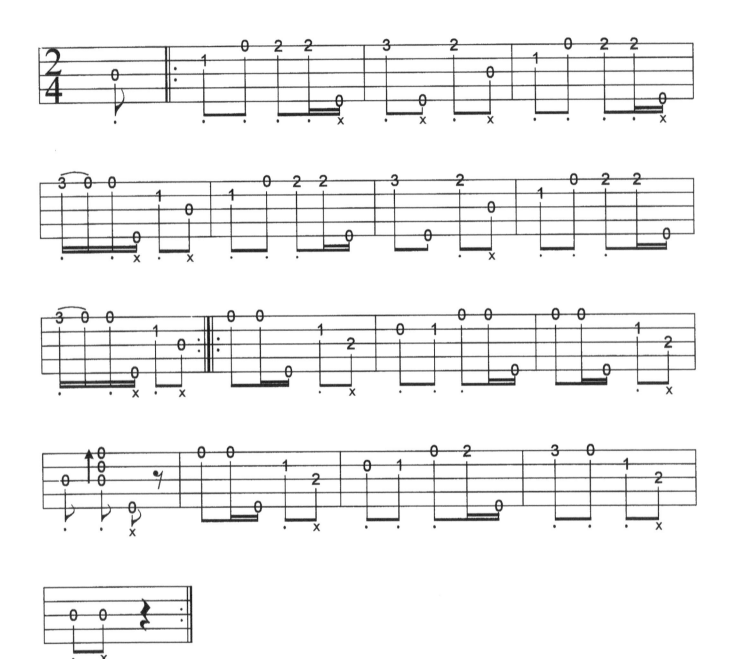

"Southern Beauty"
No. 720

No. 720 Howard "Southern Beauty" Banjo—An elegant instrument, both in appearance and musical qualities; the tone is very fine, and sure to give the most critical the very best of satisfaction in every way; instrument is fretted perfectly and true in all positions. 11 inches diameter, finest selected calf head, handsome mahogany neck, finished in natural color, with elegantly hand carved heel, and fine scroll headpiece veneered with three layers of colored wood beautifully inlaid with various designs of pearl, ebony fingerboard, pearl position dots, edged with celluloid; metal covered rim, heavily nickel-plated, inside veneered with bird'seye maple, double wired edge, straining hoop with groove for brackets to prevent cutting of head, 30 professional brackets, nickel-plated with safety nut, fastened to rim with bolts, patent neck brace, common sense metal tailpiece, and champion patent nonslipping pegs. Shipping weight, 12 lbs. Price,..$28.00

Early Banjo Advertisements

HARD TIMES

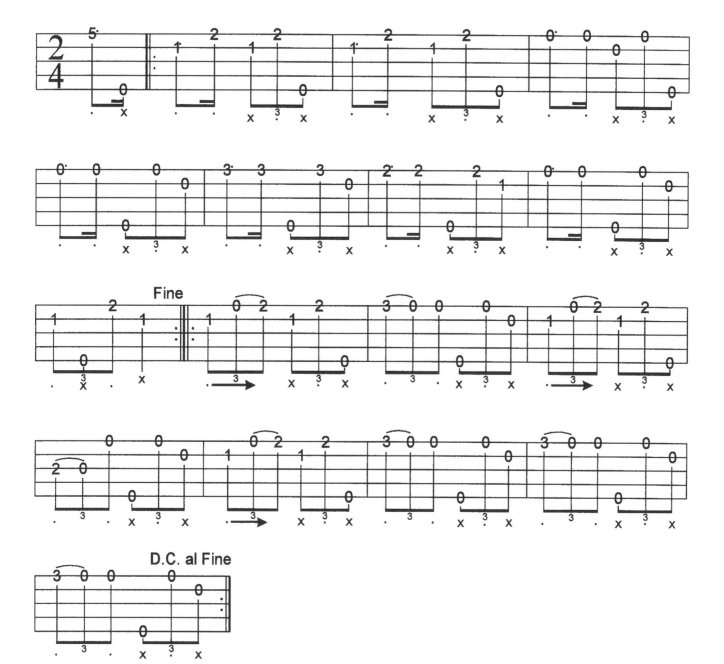

"Artist"

No. 721

No. 721 Howard "Artist" Banjo—Has all the necessary qualities required in a solo instrument; the tone is delightful and pleasing; has wonderful carrying power and is an excellent instrument for both soloist and professional; 11 inch diameter, solid mahogany neck, with fancy hand carved heel, finest quality ebony fingerboard inlaid with various designs of pearl ornaments to mark the different positions, 22 German silver frets, fingerboard bound with celluloid, full 3 octaves solid brass, heavily plated milled straining hoop, with individual groove for each bracket, a feature which has done away with the possibility of cutting the head, neck is fastened with patent metal neck adjuster, has finest quality selected calf head, nickel-plated tailpiece, champion nonslipping pegs. The biggest bargain ever offered. Shipping weight, 12 lbs. Price..$38.00

Early Banjo Advertisements

INJIN RUBBER OVERCOAT

JIM ALONG JOSEY

JIM CRACK CORN

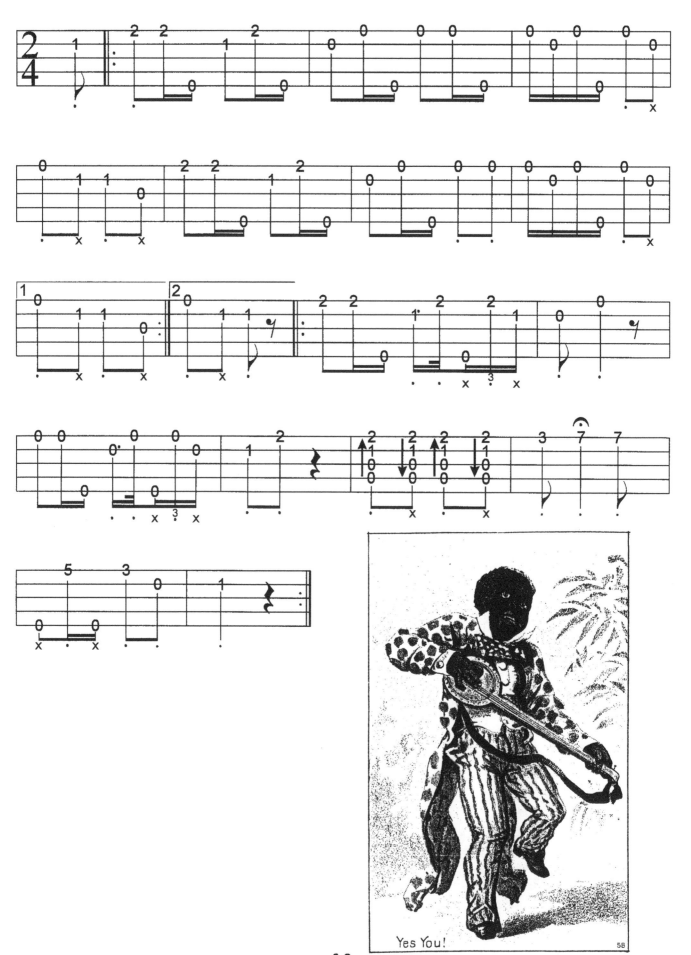

Yes You!   58

JIM CROW POLKA

JORDAN IS A HARD ROAD

KEEMO KIMO

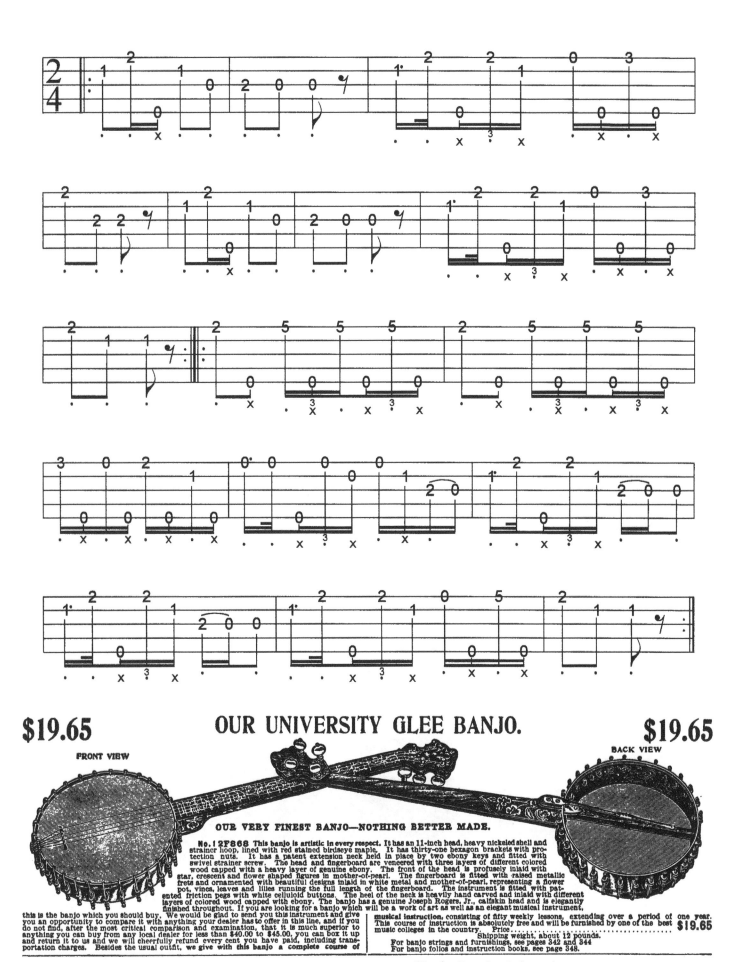

41

KICK UP DE DEBBLE ON A HOLIDAY

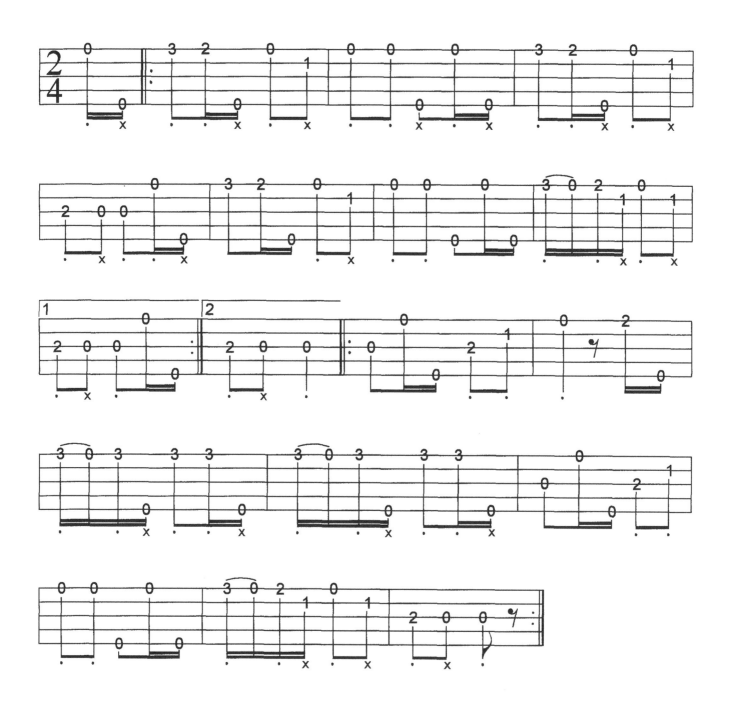

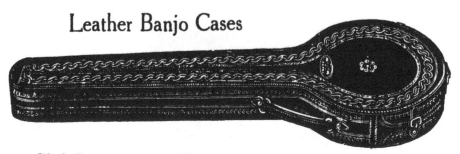

Leather Banjo Cases

Black, Russet, Orange or Wine Smooth Grain Leather, Flannel Lined, nicely Embossed, top and bottom Solid Leather. **Price $7.50**

Early Banjo Advertisements

LUCY LONG POLKA

LUCY NEAL

MARY BLANE

MISS LUCY LONG

NEBER DO TO GIB IT UP SO

NIGGA FROM DE SOUTH

OLD DAN TUCKER

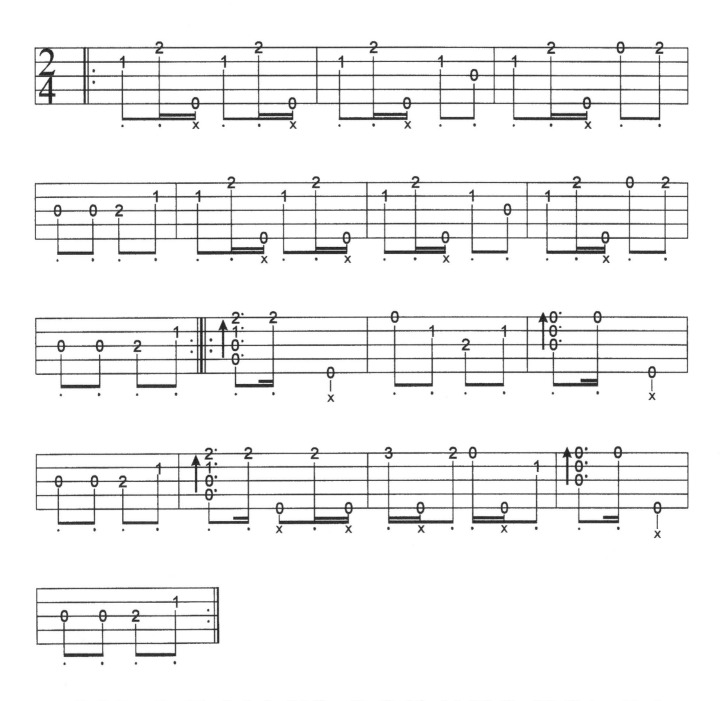

OLD DINAH'S GOIN' TO TOWN

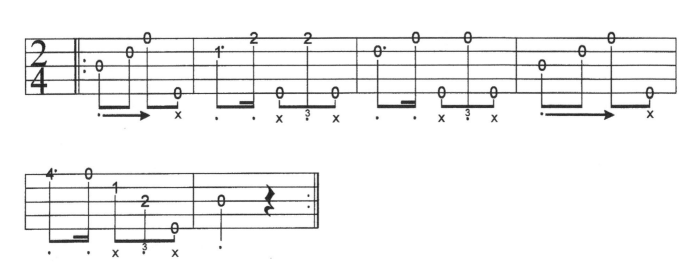

OLD JOE

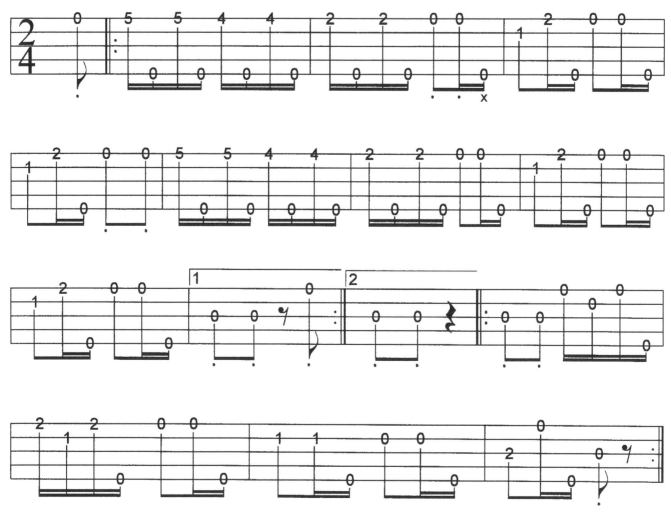

OLD JOHNNY BOKER

OLD KING CROW

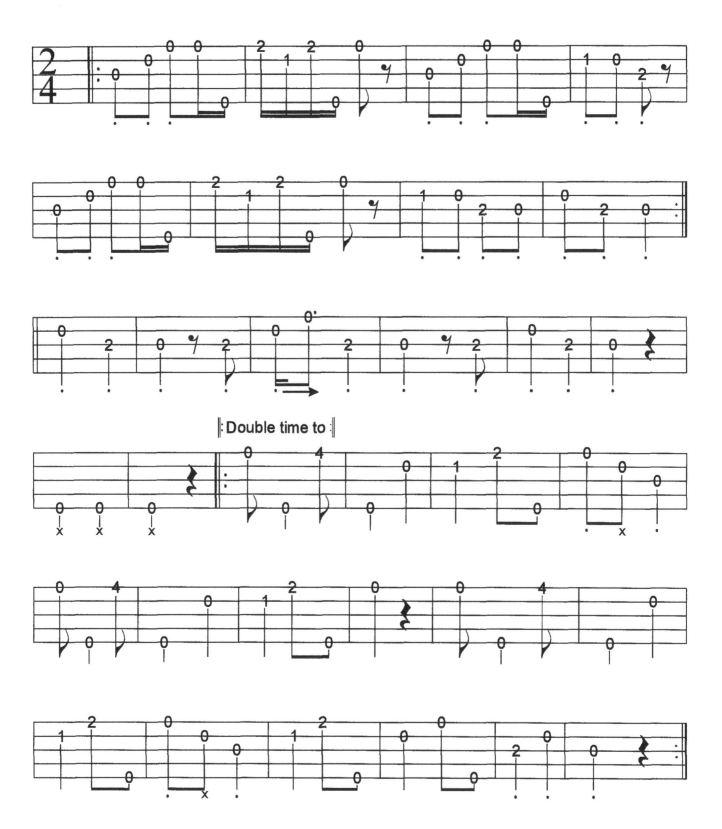

‖: Double time to ‖

OLD '76 (REEL)

OLD ZIP COON

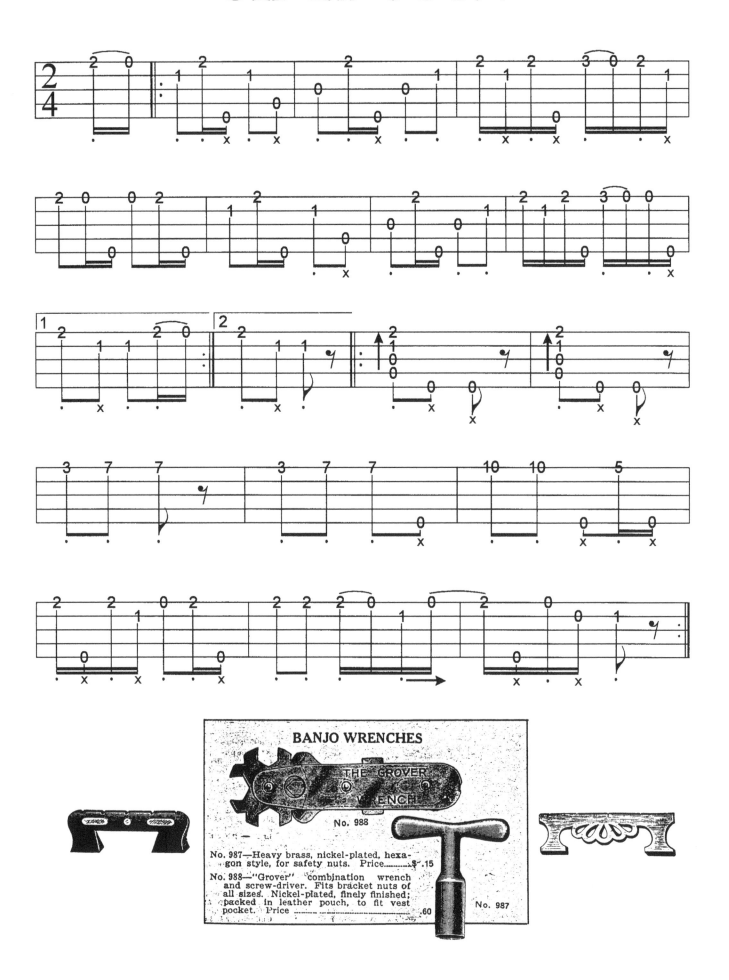

O! LUD GALS

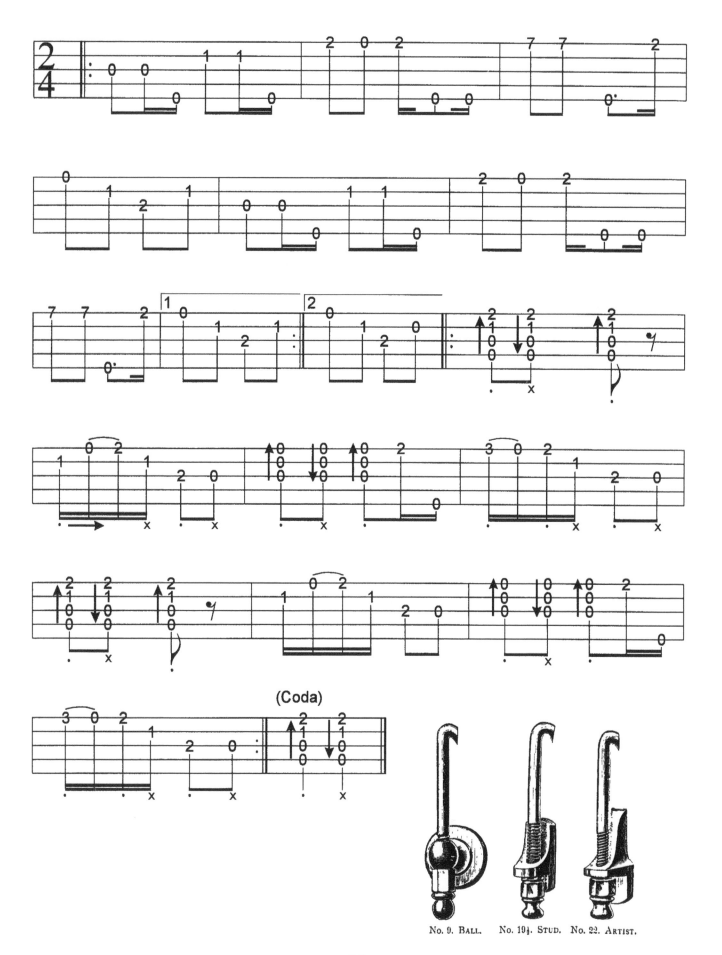

No. 9. BALL.   No. 19½. STUD.   No. 22. ARTIST.

O! PRAY GOODY

PITCH BURGUNDY PLASTER

PHILADELPHIA REEL

POP GOES THE WEASEL

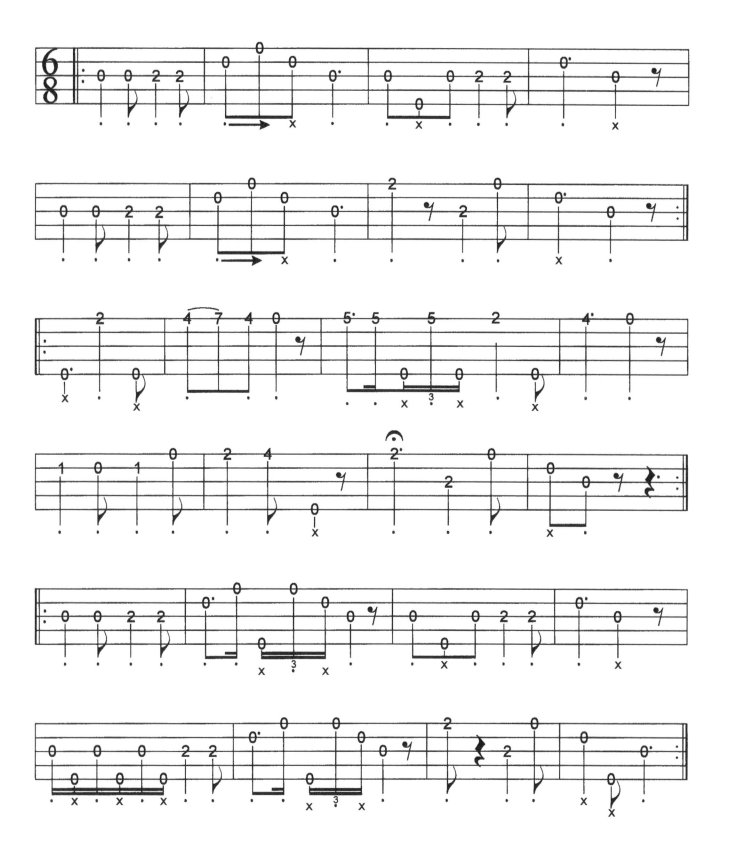

ROSA LEE

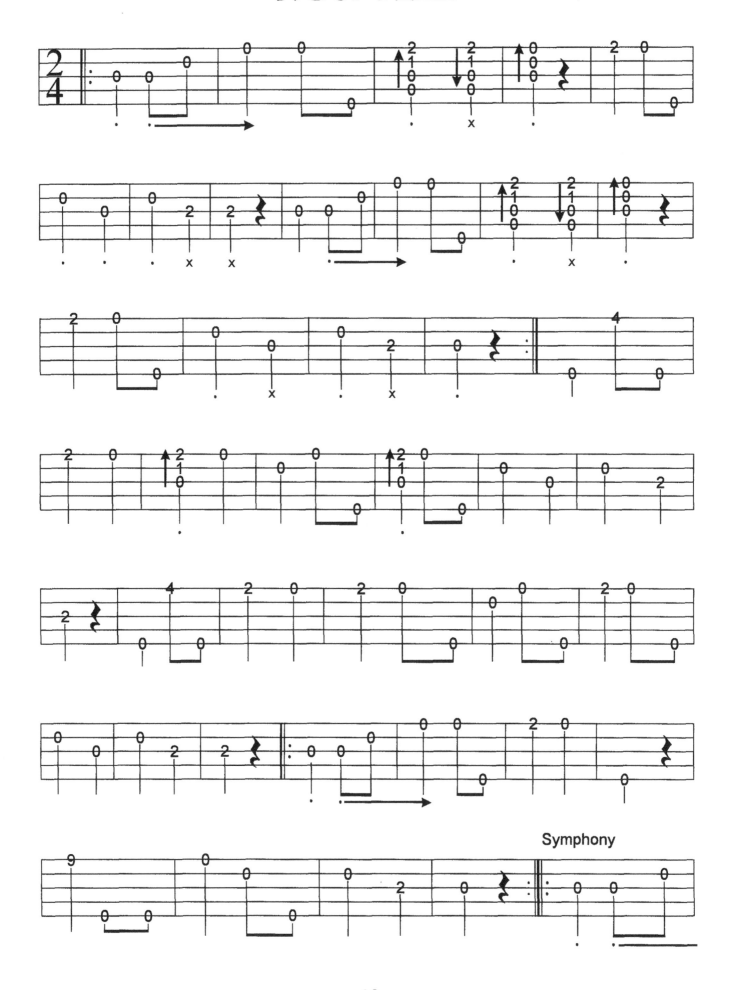

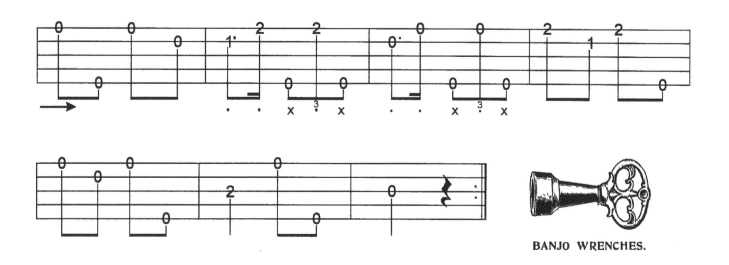

BANJO WRENCHES.

SEBASTOPOL BREAKDOWN

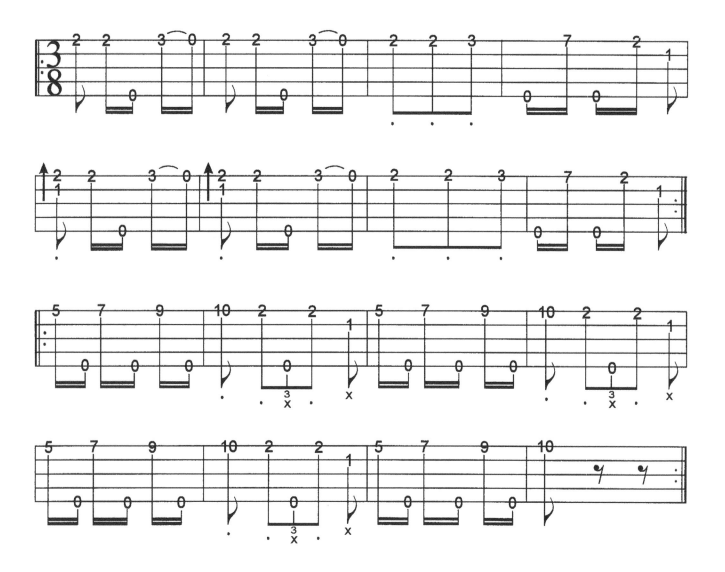

SPANISH GALLOPADE
(WITH VARIATIONS)

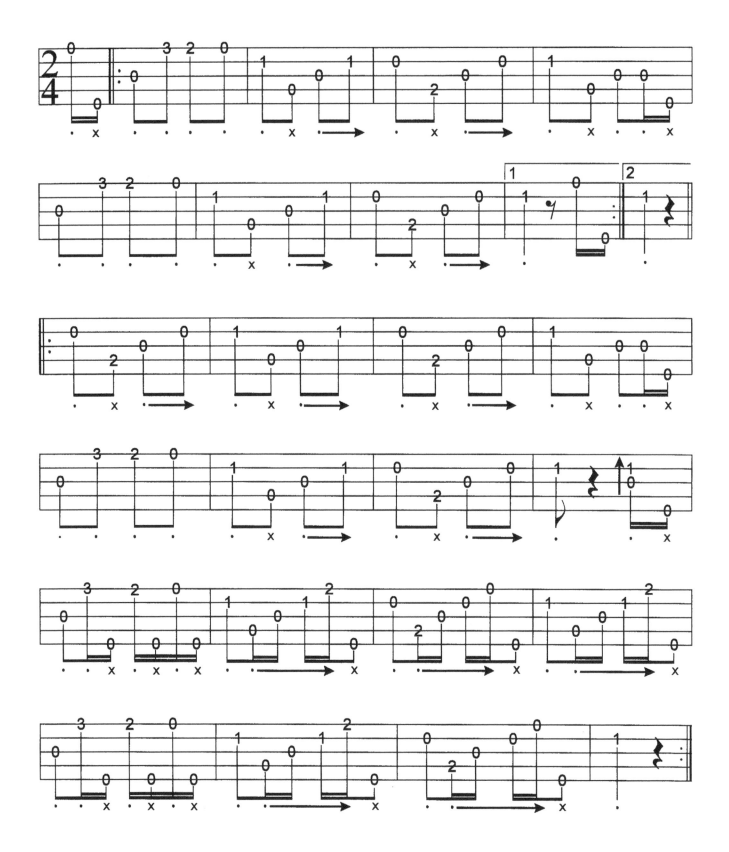

THIS SIDE OF JORDAN

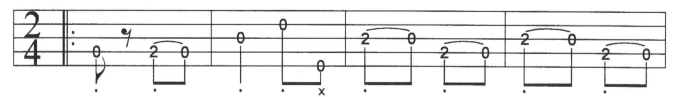

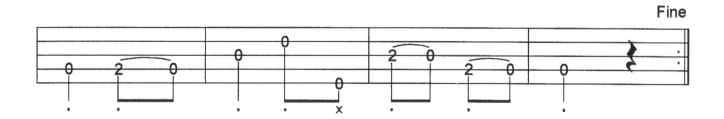

Fine

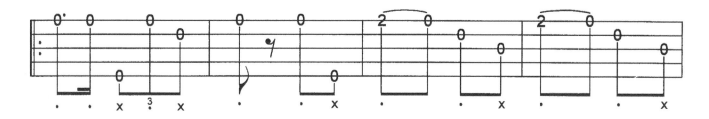

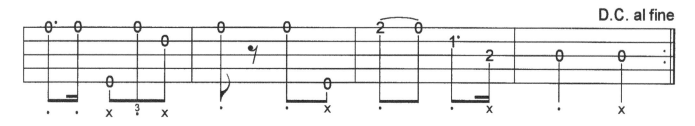

D.C. al fine

WAIT FOR THE WAGON

WALK ALONG JOHN

WALK INTO DE PARLOR JIG

WHO'S DAT A KNOCKIN'
AT DE DOOR

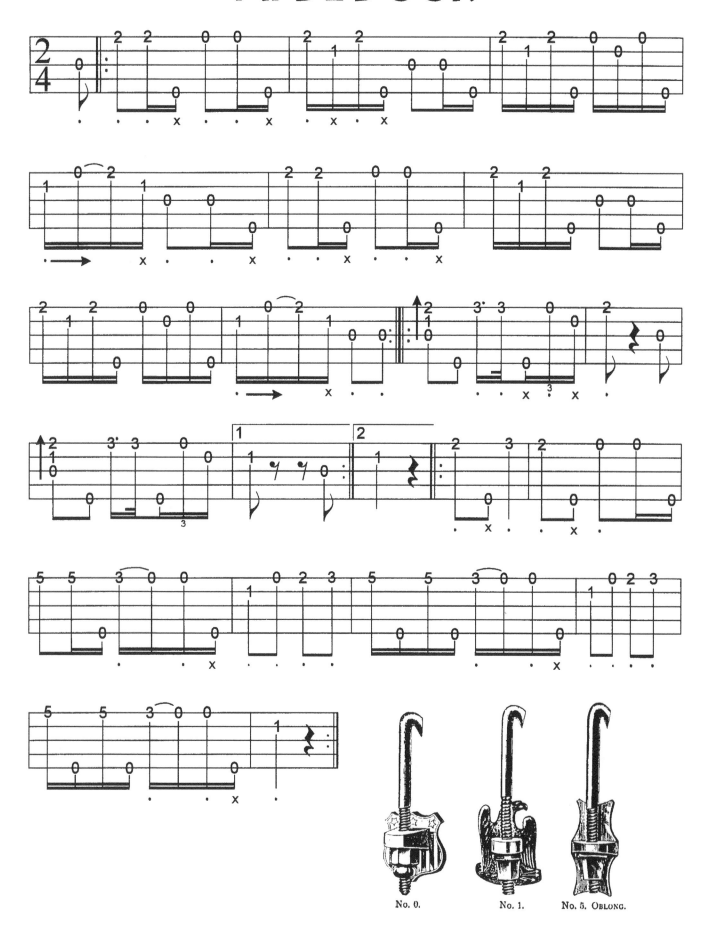

YANKEE DOODLE
(WITH VARIATIONS)

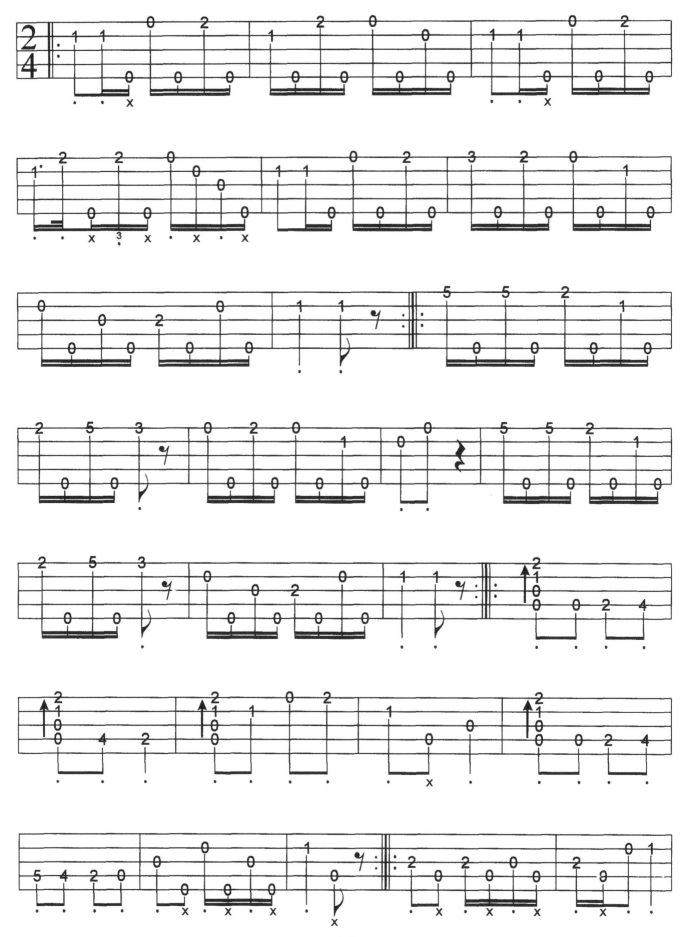

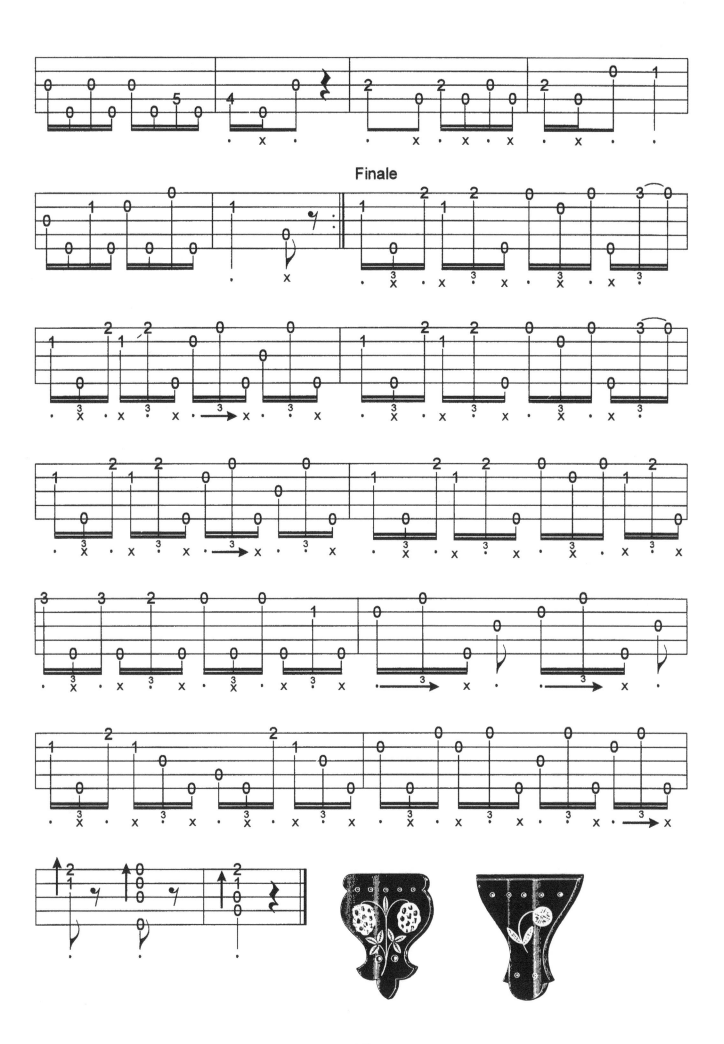

Finale

The Banjo Lesson, 1893
Henry Ossawa Tanner

This minstrel five-string (fretless) banjo is made of maple.
Manufacture comes from an identification penned onto the
reverse of the skin head in a strong 19th-century hand:
Henry P. Stichter Maker/Nov. 26th 1848.
- James F. Bollman Collection

"The Last Visitor", no doubt keen for a quiet stretch of beach at the end of the season, receives an enthusiastic welcome for some underemployed minstrels in a scene drawn in the late 1880s.

More Great Banjo Books from Centerstream...

400 SMOKIN' BLUEGRASS BANJO LICKS

by Eddie Collins

Know only 20 solo licks? How about 50? 100? 200? If that's all, then you need this book, designed to help you improvise bluegrass style solos. 400 licks are played over standard chord progressions; the use of licks sometimes will take precedent over stating the melody. The progressions used are based primarily on common vocal numbers. Some of the licks included are: chromatic licks, embellishing a fiddletune, high position licks, Reno style, pentatonic blues, boogie licks, swing phrasing, sequential licks, back-up licks and many more. Uses standard G tuning. Companion book: 400 Smokin Bluegrass Guitar Licks (#00123172).
00123175 Book/CD Pack..$19.99

GIBSON MASTERTONE
Flathead 5-String Banjos of the 1930's and 1940's
by Jim Mills

While Gibson produced literally thousands of banjos prior to WWII, only 250 or so featured that "Magic Combination" of an Original Flathead Tonering and Five-string neck. 19 of the absolute best are featured here. With details of their known histories and provenances, as well as never-before-seen photos, bills of sale, factory shipping ledgers, and other ephemera relating to these rare and highly desirable instruments..
00001241 Full Color Softcover $45.00

FORTY GOSPEL GREATS FOR BANJO
by Eddie Collins

When you hear the term "Gospel Banjo," many assume we are talking about tunes you hear at every bluegrass festival-tunes in the Southern Gospel tradition. While these definitely make for good banjo fare, Eddie sought to cover new ground, of the 40 popular songs included, nearly 20 of them have not been previously arranged for banjo, plus lyrics have been placed below each melody note to give the player a sense of when to stress notes in order to bring out the melody above the fill-notes of the rolls. Each song is played on the enclosed CD. These 40 Gospel Greats for Banjo are both enjoyable and inspirational.
00001497 Book/CD Pack..$19.99

CELTIC SONGS FOR THE TENOR BANJO
37 Traditional Songs and Instrumentals
by Dick Sheridan

Jigs & reels, hornpipes, airs, dances and more are showcased in this exciting 37 collection drawn from Ireland, Scotland, Wales, Cornwall, Brittany and the Isle of Man. Each traditional song – with its lilting melody and rich accompaniment harmony – has been carefully selected and presented for tenor banjo in both note form and tablature with chord symbols and diagrams. Lyrics and extra verses are included for many songs. Includes: All Through The Night, Blackbird Will You Go, The Campbells Are Coming, Garry Owen, Harvest Home, O'Gallaher's Frolics, Saddle The Pony, Swallow Tail Jig and many more.
00122477...$14.99

OLD TIME STRING BAND BANJO STYLES

by Joseph Weidlich

POld Time String Band Banjo Styles will introduce you to the traditional, rural string band banjo styles as played in the southern mountains of the eastern United States, which were used to "second" vocal songs and fiddle tunes during the Golden Age of recorded string band music, from the early 1920s through the early 1930s. Includes: Historical Background , String Band Transcriptions of Selected Backups and Solos, Building a Thumb-lead Style Backup.
00123693...$19.99

TRAD JAZZ FOR TENOR BANJO
by Dick Sheridan

Part of a universal repertoire familiar to all traditional jazz musicians, the 35 standards in this collection are arranged for the tenor banjo but chord symbols make playing suitable for all banjo tunings as well as other chord instruments. Popular keys have been chosen, with melodies in notes and tab, plus large, easy-to-read chord diagrams, lyrics, commentary and more. Includes: Margie, Wabash Blues, Tishmigo Blues, Avalon, Shine, Back Home Again in Indiana, Shinny like My Sister Kate, St. Louis Blues, Jazz Me Blues, Old Green River, By and By, Yellow Dog Blues and more.
00139419 Book/CD Pack..$19.99

BOB CARLIN - FIDDLE TUNES FOR CLAWHAMMER BANJO

by Bob Carlin

Renowned instructor and Grammy nominee Bob Carlin is one of the best-known banjoists performing today. This book, an update of his 1983 classic with the welcome addition of a CD, teaches readers how to play 32 best-loved pieces from his first two solo recordings: Fiddle Tunes for Clawhammer Banjo and Where Did You Get That Hat? Includes fantastic photos from throughout Bob's career.
00001327 Book/CD Pack..$19.99

GOSPEL BANJO
arranged by Dennis Caplinger

Features 15 spiritual favorites, each arranged in 2 different keys for banjo. Includes: Amazing Grace, Crying Holy, I'll Fly Away, In the Sweet By and By, Just a Closer Walk with Thee, Life's Railway to Heaven, Nearer My God to Thee, Old Time Religion, Swing Low, Sweet Chariot, Wayfaring Stranger, Will the Circle Be Unbroken, more!
00000249...$12.95

5 STRING BANJO NATURAL STYLE
No Preservatives
by Ron Middlebrook

Now available with a helpful play-along CD, this great songbook for 5-string banjo pickers features 10 easy, 10 intermediate and 10 difficult arrangements of the most popular bluegrass banjo songs. This book/CD pack comes complete with a chord chart.
00000284...$17.95

P.O. Box 17878 - Anaheim Hills, CA 92817
(714) 779-9390   www.centerstream-usa.com